Contents

Some words are printed in bold, **like this**. You can find out what they mean in the glossary.

Do You Know Someone with Allergies?

You might have a friend with an allergy. When people have allergies, their bodies are harmed by things that do not harm people without allergies.

Cat hair can make an allergic person's eyes itch, swell, get red, and water.

I Know Someone with
Allergies

Vic Parker

Heinemann Library
Chicago, Illinois

www.heinemannraintree.com
Visit our website to find out more information about Heinemann-Raintree books.

To order:

☎ Phone 888-454-2279

💻 Visit www.heinemannraintree.com to browse our catalog and order online.

Edited by Rebecca Rissman, Daniel Nunn and Siân Smith
Designed by Joanna Hinton Malivoire
Picture research by Mica Brancic
Originated by Capstone Global Library
Printed in the United States of America by Worzalla Publishing

14 13 12 11 10
10 9 8 7 6 5 4 3 2 1

Library of Congress Cataloging-in-Publication Data
Parker, Victoria.
  I know someone with allergies / Vic Parker.
    p. cm. — (Understanding health issues)
  Includes bibliographical references and index.
  ISBN 978-1-4329-4555-8 (hc)
  ISBN 978-1-4329-4571-8 (pb)
  1. Allergy—Juvenile literature. I. Title.
  RC585.P38 2011
  616.97—dc22   2010026409

Acknowledgments
We would like to thank the following for permission to reproduce photographs: Alamy pp. 6 (© Purestock/ Steve Smith), 7 (© Bubbles Photolibrary), 15 (© Kari Marttila); Corbis pp. 4 (© cultura), 14 (© Image Source); Getty pp. 17 (Blend Images/Granger Wootz), 18 (Photodisc/Matthias Tunger), 22 (Brand X Pictures/ Sarah M. Golonka), 23 (Science Photo Library/Ian Adene), 25 (Getty Images Sport/Clive Brunskill); Getty Images News p. 24 (Bongarts/Friedemann Vogel); iStockphoto pp. 10 (© Jill Chen), 13 (© Grzegorz Kula), 16 (© Tomaz Levstek), 20 (© Monika Adamczyk); Photolibrary p. 26 (Fotosearch value); Science Photo Library pp. 5 (Ian Boddy), 11 (Edwige), 21 (Coneyl Jay); Shutterstock pp. 12 (© Blaj Gabriel), 19 (© Quayside), 27 (© Paulaphoto).

Cover photograph of a woman sneezing reproduced with permission of Getty Images (Cultura/Colin Hawkins).

We would like to thank Matthew Siegel and Ashley Wolinski for their invaluable help in the preparation of this book.

Every effort has been made to contact copyright holders of any material reproduced in this book. Any omissions will be rectified in subsequent printings if notice is given to the publisher.

All the Internet addresses (URLs) given in this book were valid at the time of going to press. However, due to the dynamic nature of the Internet, some addresses may have changed, or sites may have changed or ceased to exist since publication. While the author and publisher regret any inconvenience this may cause readers, no responsibility for any such changes can be accepted by either the author or the publisher.

Someone with a **severe** allergy can wear a bracelet or necklace to let others know.

You cannot usually tell that people have allergies just by looking at them. People's bodies only show allergies when they are around the things they are allergic to. We call these things **allergens**.

What Is an Allergic Reaction?

Our bodies try to fight off harmful things, such as colds and coughs, by making special chemicals inside us called **antibodies**.

Some harmful **infections** can make you sneeze.

People can sneeze because of allergies, rather than because of an infection.

When people meet something they are allergic to, their bodies think it is harmful and make antibodies to fight it. These antibodies build up, causing bad effects. This is an **allergic reaction**.

What Can People Be Allergic To?

There are lots of things people can be allergic to. Some of these things are shown in the table below.

Allergens you can touch or that can touch you	• rubber • grass • pet hair • detergent • bee/wasp/hornet stings
Allergens you can breathe in	• dust • plant **pollen** • molds • perfume • cigarette smoke
Allergens you can swallow	• medicine • milk • fish • strawberries • sesame seeds

Allergens can affect people in different ways. People with a strong peanut allergy might become sick by eating a peanut, or even by touching one. They could even become sick just by breathing in tiny pieces of peanut.

STOP! nut free zone

please do not bring nuts into this area

You can help children who are allergic to nuts by not taking things with nuts in to school.

Who Has Allergies?

Anyone can develop allergies at any time. Nobody knows why some people get certain allergies. However, some allergies, like peanut allergy, are becoming more common.

Allergies seem to run in families.

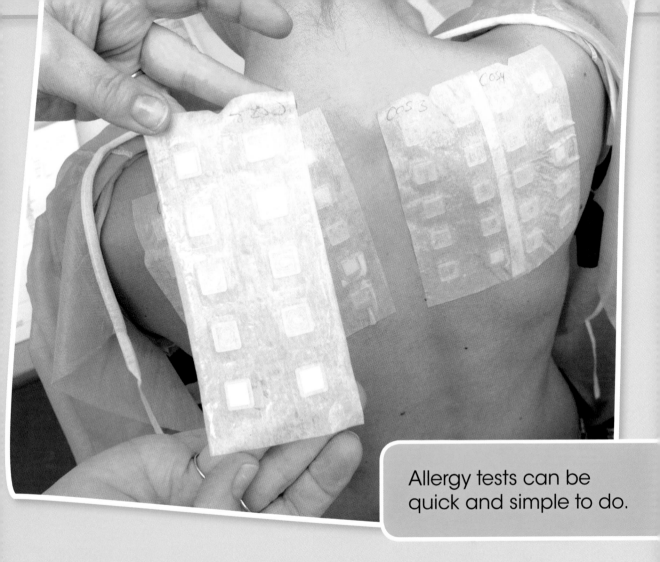

Allergy tests can be quick and simple to do.

It is usually simple for doctors or nurses to find out if someone is allergic to something. There are easy tests they can do on someone's blood or skin.

Living with Allergies

People can be given allergens as injections, tablets, or drops under their tongue.

A doctor can try to **cure** someone of an allergy by giving the person lots of very tiny amounts of the **allergen**. But this only works in some cases. No one knows why.

For most people, the only way to deal with their allergies is to keep away from the things that they are allergic to. Then they will not have **allergic reactions**.

You can help a friend with an allergy to **pollen** by playing indoors when the **pollen count** is high.

Avoiding Allergens

For many people, it can be hard to avoid **allergens**. For instance, dust and grass are often all around us. People can be bothered by this sort of allergy a lot of the time.

Allergies can be constantly irritating.

This boy has had an allergic reaction to a hornet sting.

Other people may have **allergic reactions** very rarely, such as when they are stung by a bee or a hornet. But these reactions can be **severe**. These people may feel worried or frightened about having these reactions.

Helping Hay Fever Sufferers

People who are allergic to grass and **pollen** might have a difficult time during spring and summer. They may have puffy, itchy eyes and a blocked or runny nose. This type of **allergic reaction** to the outdoors is called hay fever.

Many plants make pollen in spring and summer. This can cause problems for people with hay fever.

People with hay fever don't have to miss out on outdoor fun if they take allergy medicine.

People with hay fever can take medicines to help their eyes and nose get better. Some of these are tablets or liquid to swallow. There are also eye and nose drops, as well as sprays to squirt up the nose.

Soothing Skin

Someone allergic to horse hair may react with hives.

People may have an **allergic reaction** to something on their skin, either in one place or all over. Hives is an itchy skin rash caused by **allergens**.

Medicines can make allergic skin reactions less itchy. Some of these are tablets or liquid you swallow. Other medicines include creams that you rub in.

Eczema is a reaction that makes skin itchy, but using special creams for eczema can help a lot.

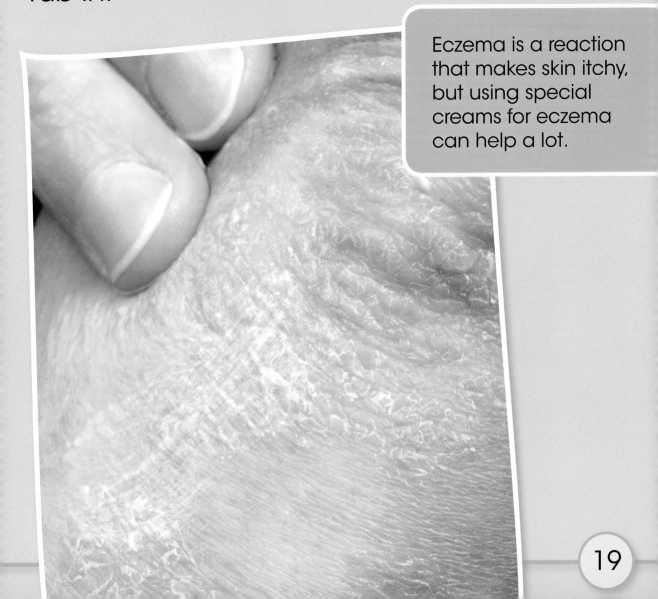

Opening Airways

People having an **allergic reaction** may start to **wheeze** and be short of breath. This happens when the airways inside their body narrow, so they cannot get enough air.

Someone might become short of breath because of an allergy to house dust.

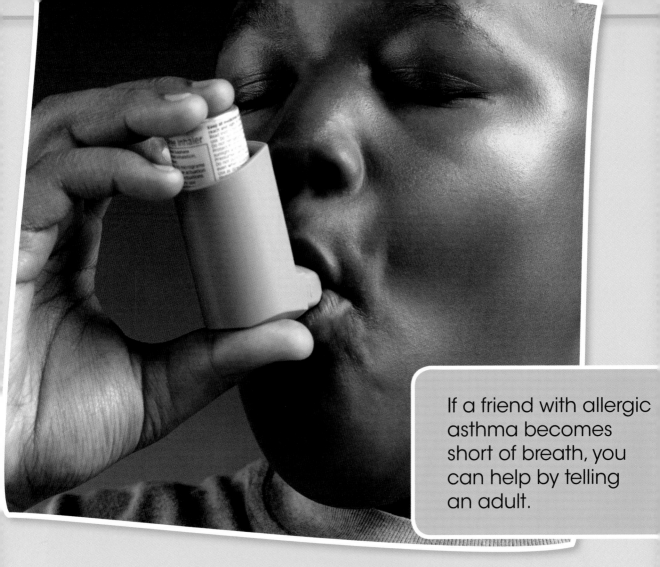

If a friend with allergic asthma becomes short of breath, you can help by telling an adult.

This type of reaction is called allergic asthma. If you have friends with allergic asthma, they may take medicine that helps them through a special spray called an **inhaler**.

Emergency!

In a **severe allergic reaction**, a person's whole body develops a rash and swells. The mouth and throat can become so swollen that airways get blocked, so the person cannot breathe. This happens extremely fast.

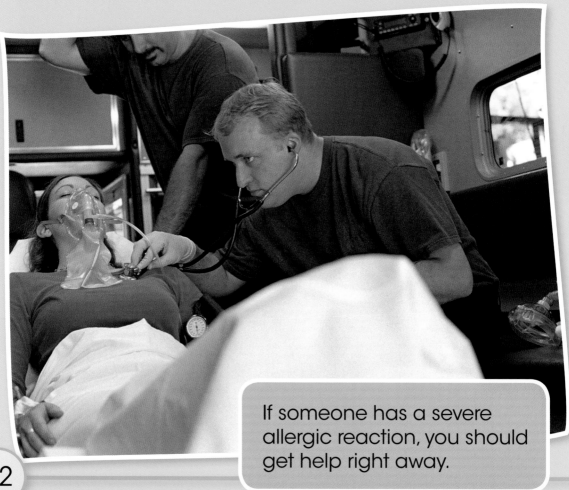

If someone has a severe allergic reaction, you should get help right away.

An injection can help people with a severe allergic reaction until they reach the hospital.

Severe allergic reactions usually happen to people who are allergic to certain foods, such as eggs. These people should always carry a special injection with them that can stop the reaction for a while.

Famous People

Lleyton Hewitt is an Australian tennis player who suffers from an allergy to grass. However, this has not stopped him from winning tennis tournaments played on grass, such as Wimbledon.

Lleyton Hewitt has shown that allergies do not have to stop you from doing what you want to do.

Serena Williams is one of the world's greatest female tennis players.

U.S. tennis superstar Serena Williams is allergic to peanuts. She is extremely fit and healthy and has won many major tournaments.

Being a Good Friend

There are many ways you can be a good friend to people with allergies. For example, you can remove anything they might be allergic to before they come to visit you.

If someone who is allergic to pet hair comes to visit, you can help by moving pets out of the room and vacuuming up any hair.

We all have different bodies and different personalities.

Living with allergies can be difficult at times. We are all different in many ways. A good friend likes us and values us for who we are.

Allergies: Facts and Fiction

Facts

- More than 3 million people in the United States have a nut or peanut allergy.

- For every 5 people around the world 1 is likely to have an allergy.

- Someone can get an allergy at any time in their life.

Fiction

(?) People with hay fever can avoid **pollen** by going out to sea.

> **WRONG!** Pollen can travel for many miles on the wind, even out to sea.

(?) You can catch allergies from other people.

> **WRONG!** You cannot catch an allergy from someone else.

(?) You cannot grow out of allergies.

> **WRONG!** You can grow out of some allergies.

Glossary

allergen something that can cause harm to someone's body, although it is not harmful to most people

allergic reaction when someone's body reacts badly to something he or she touches, breathes, eats, or drinks

antibody something our bodies make in our blood to fight off germs and keep us well

cure medical treatment that makes someone better

infection illness caused by germs

inhaler small piece of equipment you use to breathe in certain medicines

pollen fine powder made by certain plants

pollen count measurement of the amount of pollen in the air

severe extremely bad

wheeze make a high, rough noise due to difficulties breathing

Find Out More

Books to Read

Powell, Jillian. *Aneil Has a Food Allergy (Like Me, Like You)*. Langhorne, Pa.: Chelsea Clubhouse, 2005.

Robbins, Lynette. *How to Deal with Allergies (Kids' Health)*. New York: PowerKids, 2010.

Royston, Angela. *Allergies (How's Your Health?)*. Mankato, Minn.: Smart Apple Media, 2009.

Websites

http://kidshealth.org/kid/asthma_basics/related/allergies.html
Visit Kids' Health to learn more about allergies.

http://kidshealth.org/teen/your_mind/friends/helping_allergies.html
Visit Kids' Health to read about food allergies.

www.aafa.org
Learn more about dealing with allergies at this website of the Asthma and Allergy Foundation of America.

Index